JOURNEY TO
Joy

JOURNEY TO *Joy*

SERVING GOD WILLINGLY AND WITHOUT EXCUSE

DOLORES JONES

LIFEWISE BOOKS

JOURNEY TO JOY
SERVING GOD WILLINGLY AND WITHOUT EXCUSE
DOLORES JONES

Copyright © 2022 Dolores Jones. All rights reserved. Except for brief quotations for review purposes, no part of this book may be reproduced in any form without prior written permission from the author.

All scriptures are taken from the KING JAMES VERSION (KJV): KING JAMES VERSION, public domain.

Published by:
LIFEWISE BOOKS
PO BOX 1072
Pinehurst, TX 77362

LifeWiseBooks.com

To contact the author: dolores-jones.com

ISBN Paperback 978-1-958820-02-5
ISBN eBook 978-1-958820-03-2

dedication

This book is dedicated to our heavenly Father. For without Him, we can (in and of ourselves) do nothing.

Thank You, Father, for Your goodness and mercy following us on this journey. We give You praise and honor for Your faithfulness.

Thank You, Jesus, for the ultimate sacrifice of dying for us.

We give all genuine acknowledgment to the Holy Spirit as the power of God. May His glory shine upon everyone who reads this book. Amen

special thanks

I would like to thank the Lord Jesus, who has kept my children Tyrell, Alexandria, and Dynesha throughout the many challenges in our life in which they suffered the most. Despite the many moves from place to place and the sacrifices they endured in sharing me with so many others who pulled on my heart and time, they still have a heart that loves.

Again, I say thank You, Jesus!

I would like to give respect to my mother, Mary Jones, who, throughout her life of seventy-five years, reminded me of the many ways I could live a simple life without compromising joy. Therefore, I thank God for her example of love for her family and strength in times of adversity.

I also would like to remember my grandmother, Nellie Walker, for her bold faith and committed life to the gospel, along with her consistent example of prayer.

And finally, thank you to my closest friend, Yulanda Parker Blackstock. No matter how many oppositions came her way, the love of God always shined through her heart..

CONTENTS

Introduction	1
CHAPTER 1 The Beginning	3
CHAPTER 2 A Leader in The Making	9
CHAPTER 3 A Mind to Work	19
CHAPTER 4 Lost in Church	29
CHAPTER 5 Saying No Without Guilt	37
CHAPTER 6 Dare to Do Something Different	47
CHAPTER 7 The Courage to Change	55
Conclusion	61
About the Author	63
Endnotes	65

INTRODUCTION

This book is inspired by God and confirmed by Scripture. No matter what you are going through, God is still in control, and no matter what it looks like, God is still there. Opposition means "something that opposes, hostile or contrary action or condition."[1] This open warfare does not discriminate.

We all have experienced some form of opposition in our lives. We have differences of opinion in our homes, on our jobs, in our churches, and even when driving while cutting someone off. The key to overcoming opposition is to stay in our lane. We must know what is expected of us and do just that. Therefore, even when opposition comes, our standard of position in the Lord will prevail (1 John 4:4).

Opposition comes in all shapes and forms, but what it all narrows down to is that it is wrapped in lies (John 8:44). "This is the day which the Lord hath made;

We will rejoice and be glad in it." (Psalm 118:24). We very easily say this verse, but do we live or believe what it says?

How we start our day will mostly likely be the way our day will end, so if we leave home and encounter someone who just doesn't care about anyone but themselves and they take your parking space, would you react or respond? Reacting is typically quick, without much thought, tense, and aggressive. But responding is thought out, calm, and generally non-threatening.

We can no longer allow our emotions to lead us. We must practice self-control (Galatians 5:23). God expects us to live up to the standards written in His Word. If we continue to allow ourselves to be moved by every negative action, we will never be able to access the greatness within us.

Distractions are the second biggest weapon of the adversary, while fear is number one. People, places, and things are the tools he uses to distract, so what's distracting you? "For the weapons of our warfare are not carnal, but mighty through God to the pulling down of strongholds." (2 Corinthians 10:4-5).

Chapter 1
THE BEGINNING

"In the beginning was the Word, and the Word was with God, and the Word was God."
John 1:1

As Mary sat at the feet of Jesus, soaking in His every word, Martha was busy doing meaningless things, and of course, to her they had meaning. I often wondered why she felt the need to run around so much and not at least take some time for herself. Her lack of prioritizing is a prime example of how we can miss an encounter with Jesus. There is a time for everything. Martha, like many of us, might not have been so frustrated with life if she had just come, sat, listened, and talked to Jesus.

Many of our lives are filled with distractions that prevent us from giving our full attention to God's will. What is distracting you" The Word of God says that if we draw near to Him, He will draw near to us (James 4:7). Our relationship with Jesus should be our number one priority, but He's often not first in our lives.

HOME SWEET HOME

When I was growing up, we were considered poor when it came to money, but we were rich when it came to family. We did many things together. I am the seventh of eleven children, and we shared everything. We were really close, not only because we had a large family, but we only had a small three-room house. Talk about crowded, but we were happy.

When I was about ten years old, our mother moved us from our tight-knit home in Mississippi to a big city in Missouri, and our family was not so close anymore. I think everyone was happy about the move, except me. My brothers and sisters played, had fun, and embraced their newfound freedom to explore and see new things.

I, on the other hand, was devastated and not thrilled at all. I wanted the closeness we once shared as a family. I missed the intimate talks and fellowship at the dinner table, and I did not know what would become of us.

During this time, even with all my family near, I felt very alone. We had all drifted apart. While they enjoyed their new adventures, my joy was staying close to Mom. I became withdrawn and distant from others. I felt a grave disconnect because I wished they could see that something was missing. I longed to hear their voices and be in their presence as we once were in our little house.

BECOMING

Even as a young child, God was calling me to be set apart for His purpose. Even now, there are too many voices speaking, and we can't hear the most important voice—God's. He is our shepherd, and we, the sheep, are called to know His voice and follow Him. When we hear about having a calling on our life, some think in reference to glamourous spiritual titles. But this simple request from our Lord just requires a little quality time, a listening ear, and an open heart to receive.

There is a void in our lives that can only be filled by a true, loving relationship with the Father. It starts by understanding God's love for us. We can't take others' word for it; this requires us to get to know Him for ourselves. God's love is in our hearts; all we need to do is believe it and then receive what comes with it.

On this journey, there will be many distractions and obstacles geared toward leading us astray. And it will not be easy keeping your mind on God every day, but He promises you it is possible (Isaiah 26:3, Matthew 24:13).

As a child, I wanted to say a lot, but I wouldn't dare. In those days, children were seen but not heard, so I quietly stayed in my lane. I didn't know what was happening to me. I saw and knew things far beyond my years and was afraid. Even though I stayed close to my mother, the fear of the unknown was still there. I began to see words appear before me, and I longed to understand their meaning.

Why was I seeing them?
Where did they come from?
What was I to do with them?

VICTORY IN TIME

Staying close to God, even when we don't understand His plan, is the key to enduring. Enduring is something that is "long-lasting and patient."[2] This, in terms of the fruit of the Spirit, is called long-suffering, and we all have conflicts with this fruit.

Whether it is praying for the salvation of a family member or time for a promotion, waiting always seems hard to do. It is a challenge, but it is necessary for growth to take place in our lives.

There were many times in my life I had to endure, and the outcome has been great, and I wondered why I was so fretful. "Do not be afraid" is commanded in the Bible 365 times and in many different phrases. We can take one of these verses each day to meditate on and walk in victory.

SIMPLY BELIEVE

Many times, we don't need anyone else to tear us down because we do a good job all by ourselves. My encouragement to us all is to not be so hard on ourselves. We need to give ourselves grace while we grow. When we are wounded, we are driven by our emotions, but when we are healed, we are driven by love.

God is patient and loving. He never changes, yet we do all the time. Take some time and look over the events of your life and see where you might have missed Him working on your behalf.

I was led to start this book, yet I still had some fears from my childhood. Because we are all still a child at heart, we often carry hurt from the past and often cover it up with anything that will keep us from feeling the pain. My choice to cover up my pain was with alcohol and entering immoral relationships. Let me assure you, this isn't the solution, and it doesn't make you happy.

This is another opposition placed in our lives, disguised as fun! The Word of God is the only thing that can free us form the bondage of pain. Sometimes we use God's Word to just get by and not for the transformational change it is designed to make in our heart. Only God's words can help access the grace He has given us to truly love others. We start by coming to Him with childlike faith, trusting that He loves us unconditionally.

Chapter 2
A LEADER IN THE MAKING

"Trust in the Lord with all thine heart; and lean not unto thine own understanding. In all thy ways acknowledge him, and he shall direct thy paths."
Proverbs 3:5-6

When it was time to start school, I was delighted because my English class was filled with words! I looked forward to our spelling test time like it was a candy treat. I had finally found a release for the words that filled my thoughts. When I was home, I desired the courage to speak and say, "Let's sit a spell and talk," but everyone was too busy. I tried to live the best way I could without the intimacy of my family, but it was very hard, lonely, and cold. I thank God for the words because, as I look back, they kept me going.

GIFT OF SIGHT

We were born to serve God with the gifts He has given us, and yes, they belong to Him. God knew us before we were conceived in our mother's womb, and He set us apart. We are destined to be different and chosen to be great. Our heart is designed to be filled with His love continually, accept it, and resist anything else.

Our body is the temple of God; everything about us was created to reverence Him. The word reverence seems to be a thing of the past in families today. Maybe it's because we might not know the meaning of the word. Reverence means "having a deep respect for someone."[3] Many times, we can't live out this meaning because we have been wounded by our earthly father or mother. My father's character was so distorted that I could barely recognize my heavenly Father.

High expectations of a father were natural for me to have, but they were placed on an imperfect father. He was not able to meet them to my satisfaction. What little he did do wasn't seen as anything. I am sure he did something worth my attention but focusing on the negative cast a dark shadow on anything good.

Once the light of God's Word comes in, we can see His truth in every area of our lives. We sometimes think of God in the same way we experienced our natural father and forget that He has been with us from the beginning.

Did you have moments as a child when God spoke to you in dreams and visions, showing you what you could be? Become it! Draw strength and courage from what He reveals to you from them and believe that they are conceivable. Nothing is impossible with God because He is still greater. I bless you with all that this and the next life has to offer.

LOVE REVEALS

Sometime later, our mom decided to move from Missouri to Illinois. This time I was very happy because this place was totally different. It was a small town, a little way from Chicago. It reminded me of back home in Mississippi. The people were so friendly compared to the city we had left—being loud and violent, always doing something, and never wanting to rest or sleep.

This new beginning was quiet and peaceful. I came out of my shell, embracing this new move and the new me. I did not make any new friends right away, but I enjoyed my siblings and cousin immensely. Another wonderful thing that happened in this new place was we started going to church, and it was an amazing adventure getting to learn the Word of God!

His Word had a greater purpose and meaning for my life than being good at spelling words from school. I absorbed them like a sponge, and they bought me great joy. I looked forward to our weekly scripture memory verse. Mr. and Mrs. Fleming were our bus driver and assistant, and they did a wonderful job preparing our hearts by singing songs and hymns before church. They planted many seeds of the Word of God in us, and I am eternally grateful to them.

Our mom wasn't going to church at that time, but she sent us every week. Sometimes we might not have the strength to do what's right for ourselves, but we can help someone else while God is working on us. He didn't call us to perfection, He called us to love, and our mom displayed this to the end.

GROWING PAINS

When we left Mississippi, I couldn't understand why and I wanted to go back, but my mom knew something we didn't. There were hardly any jobs for a woman with eleven children except picking cotton or cucumbers for pay. I think I was eating as many cucumbers as I was picking, which explains why I love pickles so much. My mom was right for moving us so that we could have a better chance at life. Looking back, she was right about many things.

Our parents were given to us for the purpose of providing guidance in a loving, nurturing way. God chose each of our parents for this task, and because we are imperfect, all we can do is our best. Seeking to understand another person's choices is part of growing in compassion, which is lacking in the world today.

As children, we tend to take everything at face value and are not willing to yield to anyone else's view if it doesn't match our own. My mom had this wonderful way of looking at life. The wisdom she expressed was not received by me until I matured.

Our mother went home to glory in 2014, and if I could have a do-over with her, I would stick close to her every day as I did when I was a child. This is what it looks like with the heart of the Father. He desires us to come to Him like a little child—trusting. Trusting is hard sometimes when all you have known is pain, but it is possible.

PRAYER WORKS

I remember when I entered a marriage to an abusive man, and I was too embarrassed to tell my mom. I found out later that if I had told her, I would have found that my dad was also abusive to her, and that too, was another reason for our departure from our hometown.

> "Confess your faults one to another, and pray one for another, that ye may be healed…"
> James 5:16

We often hold back things from our children about our past because of shame, but this only leaves them vulnerable to the same predators. I would like to think that if I had known about this act of betrayal before, maybe I would have been more alert to the signs. I am not blaming anyone for my choices, what I'm saying is there comes a time when we should be willing to share with our family the truth about things that hurt us.

Some family members may not want to accept what you tell them about your pain but take their response to the Lord. When you share your past, if those hearing it are in denial, the door is still open until someone in the family closes it. That someone might be you!

Agree with God to heal not only you but everyone involved. Pray His will be done in your situation, and know that God has a plan for even those who have caused affliction in your life to become someone better.

> "...The effectual fervent prayer of a righteous man availeth much."
> James 5:16

Effectual fervent in Greek is *energeo*. It means "to be operative, be at work, and put forth power."[4] We must not wait until a situation arises in our life to pray. I have been moved by the Holy Spirit to pray, years in advance, for my children and grandchildren. Yet, I am still waiting for some of those prayers to be answered.

Some answers or manifested results come instantaneously, and some take time depending upon our faith and God's timing. Let me assure you that if you have not been praying, you can start where you are right now. It's never too late to start a new beginning in any area of your life.

TAKE A DEEP BREATH

Another example of me experiencing a new beginning was when I was transferred to a new school. Upon my arrival, I was approached by a girl who asked my name, and I told her. I was excited because I thought she wanted to be my friend, but I was dead wrong. She had another agenda and tried to provoke me to fight. I resisted for a while until I got fed up, and we fought.

Without knowing it, I had given my authority to her, and she used it against me. God's way of dealing with conflict is not the way we usually choose to solve it. That was my first and last fight. Our principal took us into his office and gave us the paddling of a lifetime. It left a lasting impression on me. That day, I learned to never give anyone that much control over my emotions.

We have been given authority, so what are we going to do with it?

Will we choose anger or authority?

We must pick our battles.

When we put expectations on others that are far beyond their compacity to meet at that time, it leads to anger. In James 3:17 it says, "But the wisdom that is from above is first pure, then peaceable, gentle, and easy to be intreated, full of mercy and good fruits, without partiality, and without hypocrisy." The entire book of James should be a guide for every leader to teach from. It covers how to use the wisdom of God for kingdom living as we keep our focus on Him.

Anger is a sign that something is wrong, not in the other person or situation, but in us. We have no right to be angry beyond the time God has graced us to be angry. That time frame is sundown (Ephesians 4:26).

When we let anger fester and grow, our attitude becomes rotten, and we are of no use to the Father at that moment. As anger rises, all the authority and power we have acquired is used against us by the adversary (1 Peter 5:8).

God's nature is quick to forgive and slow to anger. He calls us to a higher standard than what we are angry about. He advises us to be quick to hear His voice in situations like this, but it takes practice to develop this skill. We can have all the education and intelligence the world has to offer, but nothing compares to using it for understanding and knowing the Lord.

Chapter 3
A MIND TO WORK

"For we are not as many, which corrupt the word of God: but as of sincerity, but as of God, in the sight of God speak we in Christ."
2 Corinthians 2:17

Deception is defined as "the act of deceiving;"[5] therefore, it takes away our choice to make a good decision. Truth is meant to make you free, and when you are free, you make better choices.

In the previous chapter, I spoke of how I married an abusive man. He didn't present himself in that manner at first. In the beginning, he was charming and loving—a perfect example of deception.

I know now that when he was growing up, he didn't plan to go around deceiving others. Before this revelation came, I was angry and couldn't see him in this light of truth. I was convinced that he intentionally hurt me, but I was wrong.

I was also wrong to think that eighteen was an appropriate age to become an adult. The world dictates it is the legal age for accountability, but if we admit it, we were not mature enough to make major life decisions alone. Thinking I was grown, the first decision-making mistake I made was I left God. The second mistake was I left the nurturing and caring presence of my mom.

Life is all about relationships, and I made the two biggest mistakes of my life before the age of twenty. Things continued to get worse after that, with one bad relationship decision after another. I wanted to be free, but I didn't understand that I was already free. All I had to do was make the right decision of listening to God and the mother who He chose to help guide me.

Galatians 3:23 tells us that before Jesus came, we were under the law until God revealed Jesus to us. This is how our life before Christ compares to our life before we were mature enough to leave our parents.

RESTORED RELATIONSHIP

Rules are everywhere, and they are meant to help keep the peace and protect us. Its original design was to maintain order through Adam. God gave him dominion and rule over everything. The key command to not eat from the forbidden tree was given to him as the first man created.

After his wife, Eve, was given to him, she took the forbidden fruit first and was blamed by Adam and many more for the fall of man. Still, today, we tend to blame others instead of accepting responsibility for our actions.

God is the ultimate ruler over everything. He lost a valued friend and companion when He mercifully kicked Adam out of the Garden of Eden. God is still all-powerful and the only true and living God we serve. Because of His great love for us, He graciously gave us Jesus so authority could be restored to us. This is what a loving father does when we accept responsibility for our actions.

If there is a problem, He presents it to us. He then waits for us to take ownership of our part in the problem. Then He lovingly leads us in the clearing of our heart to make room for His love that covers our sin (1 Peter 4:8).

THERE IS HELP IN UNBELIEF

The adversary has a hatred for God and anything He loves and is out to destroy it (John 10:10). He will use anything and anyone to complete his mission of keeping the children of God from having an intimate relationship with the Father. He will lie, cheat, and steal to get us off track, until we've made our home in hell with him. Satan doesn't do this simply because misery loves company, he does this to hurt the Father's heart.

The Father has a plan, and that plan is Jesus. He sent Jesus to die for our sins, and now no matter what sin we commit, it's covered. The blood of Jesus is flowing down all around us like a mural painted on a wall. It surrounds us like a shield protecting and at the same time, allowing our Father to see us through the eyes of Jesus.

Nothing can distort God's view of us. He is positioned on the throne, which is the best seat in the house. Jesus's blood is applied to all our lives, and His death, burial, and resurrection are the perfect representation of how much God loves us. It is easy to think that this special gift of Jesus's blood is just for the perfect or the most elect, but it is for everyone—the just and the unjust (Matthew 5:45).

We have been lied to, and it has caused great division among us as women leaders, and the greater works of Jesus are in danger. We have failed miserably at working together and we are still failing, but today is a new day, new year, and a new beginning. Let's begin again, first by remembering Jesus!

SENT TWO BY TWO

We must love to be effective in working together; we have pretended long enough that we care about each other. We often speak about teamwork, but a team is not a group of people who just work together. A team is a group of people who learn how to trust each other. Only the grace of God can help us to walk in this kind of harmony.

As aged women of God, we are commanded to teach younger women how to love (Titus 2:3-5). The titles we carry are just words unless we use them with the right motive, seeing them as an honor and privilege from God while wearing them. They are not for show or performance but to bring glory to God because nothing we have belongs to us.

The harvest is plentiful with young women who are hungry themselves for what we have been given. We all have different gifts, and our strengths lie in allowing each of us to flow in them the way the Lord has designed.

God created every person to carry out His purpose in the world. He equips each one of us with unchangeable features that allow us to achieve His will. Among them are limitations and disabilities that require us to access His power (2 Corinthians 12:9).

THE TIME IS NOW

There is power in unity. It has been said many times that women can't work together. I am asking you to take a stand and speak life into your fellow sister in Christ. Tear down those walls that keep us divided and learn from the book of Nehemiah about how to work together effectively. Nehemiah didn't waver in his faith that God would provide all that he needed, especially who to work with in rebuilding the temple. Your ministry is in the heart of God, and He wants to guide you, just seek Him.

When Nehemiah asked about the temple from his hometown, the answer wasn't what he expected. After hearing about the destruction of the temple, he was saddened, then soon after, he fasted, prayed, and repented. It's normal when you hear bad news to become sad or even mad, but we are not to stay in that place. Nehemiah quickly moved from one phase to the next because he had a close intimate relationship with God.

He knew why this happened to his people, and when he repented, it was for himself as well as his people. Sometimes it's not just about us. Let's get over ourselves and look around to see who needs us.

There is no need for jealousy because there are plenty of souls to go around that need saving. You are valued, and you have worth; go share that with a young lady. Don't just say you will pray for them, pray for them diligently. You may be the only one praying for them.

Find someone who can't do anything for you and do all you can for them as the Lord leads. Many people ask me why I give by helping people. I simply answer because it was given to me freely (Matthew 10:8).

God gave His Son to help me, now I give my life to help others. This is the greater work Jesus speaks of that we should continue. I say again, it is not about you or me, it's all about Him, and if we are not fully persuaded about this we are walking in error. How many passages have we read or heard confirming this very message with things like learn of me, imitate me, follow me?

REDIRECTED FOCUS

I wasn't totally persuaded myself until I was diagnosed with breast cancer in 2018. Even though the Lord assured me it wasn't my time, I was led to a place of reflecting over my life and found myself wondering what if it was my time. What did I have to leave my children and grandchildren? I had concluded that whatever I thought of wasn't enough at that moment. Yes, I was thinking about money at first and it didn't stop there. Money was not the main thing I needed to leave for them; I needed to leave them Faith in God!

I set out on a journey and started leading my family. I had been leading other people's children since 2003. I had this misguided thinking that while I'm doing God's work, He will do what needs to be done with them. No one taught me this, but when I started to ask the Lord why this was happening because it doesn't make sense. He soon gave me an answer, "Charity begins at home" (1 Timothy 5:8).

Now I am a leader of my own children, and I am seeing great manifestations of the glory of God. This journey has been a long one with little pieces of progress appearing at different times over the years. It takes time and patience working with faith to see the desired change you need to see in you and the person you are praying for. It will always begin in you first, so let's start by saying, "God help me" in place of "Lord, help them."

I've found that praying this way not only takes the plank out of my own eye, but also gives me grace until the other person can come to the place of allowing theirs to be pulled out. My friend, Yulanda, showed this type of love and grace as we walked together, and she never wavered in having patience with me. I now look back on those times to encourage me and help me persevere with patience.

We often forget what it took for someone to bear our burdens before we surrendered to God, and it shows when we give up on others. I was there and so were you, so allow yourself to remember who helped you (Matthew 11:28). Use how they impacted your life to make a difference in someone else's life. This is what the cycle of life looks like in the spiritual realm of God's kingdom (John 13:34-35). Love is the greatest commandment.

Chapter 4
LOST IN CHURCH

"Come unto me, all ye that labour and are heavy laden, and I will give you rest. Take my yoke upon you, and learn of me; for I am meek and lowly in heart: and ye shall find rest unto your souls. For my yoke is easy, and my burden is light."
Matthew 11:28-30

Submission is a voluntary thought process that comes from the heart. Most of us often begin submitting in actions, doing the things that are visible to the eyes of man. God calls us to submit our hearts to Him first. He will then guide us in the direction of serving His people in love. If our motive is not genuine, our serving will be in vain. When we humble ourselves, elevation will surely come. We belong to God; therefore, all glory goes to Him—every word and every deed (1 Corinthians 6:20).

I remember when I did not know what I would do without church, and I soon started to find out. One day, I went to church for Sunday school as I faithfully did. The teacher passed out an assignment sheet and on it was the question, "Why do you go to church?" We were to take it home, answer it, and bring it back the following Sunday for discussion. I was so excited because I could think of a lot of wonderful reasons why I went to church. It was almost too many to name.

When the day came for me to sit down and answer this question, my spirit was not at peace about anything that came to my mind. I couldn't understand what was happening. Surely, I had one good, godly reason for going to church! I continued to sit, hoping that something would come from my heart that pleased God for me to write and…NOTHING!

I couldn't think of one solid foundational reason why I went to church every Sunday and every Wednesday night Bible study and every time in between for eight years. My heart was crushed and grieved at the fact that I had no answer. The tears began to flow, leading me to a place of repentance.

I had failed God once again on this journey, but this time I knew what to do, and it was not to hide from Him. It was to draw closer, seeking His presence more than ever before in my life. When drawing nearer to God, first ask Him to help you breathe. Then ask the Holy Spirit to come alive in you and help you clearly see the work that needs to be done.

We should not be ashamed to admit that we don't know what to pray for. Ask the Holy Spirit to intercede. Ask for your thoughts to be renewed for His purpose. God is our keeper, and He will keep you if you want to be kept.

STAYING CONNECTED

Our commitment to God requires us to embrace the deity of who He is to us, joined in oneness with Him. We cannot get the full revelation of His deity without surrendering our all to Christ. There is no other way to get to God except through your life being submitted to following Christ. Only Jesus can reveal the Father to us. Just saying, "I know God," or "I believe in God" is not enough (Matthew 11:27).

Sometimes we will develop this half-hearted belief about Jesus as the Son of God and Him as God, but He is the truth, the way, and the life (John 14:6-11). No matter how we sugar coat it, Jesus is the only way to the Father. No shortcuts are allowed.

Jesus got the short end of the stick since before He was born. He was almost abandoned by His earthly father, Joseph. He was almost murdered by King Herod at birth. He was lost on a journey with His parents. All this before He was thirteen years old.

Most of us have experienced a painful journey in our own way, and the Father is saying to us, "I know your pain, and I see your hurt. Give it to me."

The enemy of God tried to take us out just like he tried with Jesus. But Jesus's death became life for us. Whatever death-like trials we are experiencing today have the potential to be life for someone else.

KNOWING IS BELIEVING

As believers, the love of God is in our hearts, and nothing can separate us from it. I was shocked and dismayed at the same time because I thought this is what the Lord required of me to do with my time. I have come to understand that He had more of Himself that He desired to reveal to me and more to come.

Many times, we want to know God without surrendering our all to Jesus or without acknowledging the Holy Spirit as the power of God that gives us life (2 Timothy 3:5-7). We cannot have our cake and eat it too; this matter is too important to be handled so immaturely. This relationship must be built on a solid foundation of knowing each One individually in order to understand the oneness They share.

Can you think of a time when others only wanted to accept a portion of who you were? We all have encountered someone we thought was not good enough to get to know. There have been many attempts of the enemy to abort divine connections through relationships. It is up to us to see the deception by resisting the first impression lie. (The truth is that you can't make a good decision about anything by looking at it one time.) This lie was designed by the adversary to keep division active, especially among women. We are now only as intimate with God as we really choose to be.

We will make mistakes, and God will continue to use them to help us learn and grow. Every trial that comes in our life is an opportunity for us to grow in hope, faith, and love. If we wish them away, we end up with dead or weak faith. As we move forward in our walk with the Lord, the voices of evil will tell us if we make a mistake, we are not worthy of God's love. This is deception at its worst, don't believe it.

TOTAL FAITH

We must not be afraid to go through trials. Blaming God while enduring them is most assuredly not the answer either. There is good in every trial. We may not always see it at the time because we are trying too hard to get out of it. Our attitude while going through trials sometimes determines how long we stay in it. If we surrender our all to Jesus and allow God to help us endure, the outcome will always be great.

What is your trial today?

Are you counting it all joy or are you murmuring and complaining?

Joy during trials does not mean that we let others misuse us. Instead, it says, "I choose me." This is not selfish. We are radiating a message out to the world that we love God. Others will see Him in your expression of joy, love, and hope, which will in turn lead them to ask what they can do to be saved.

You receive all the treasures of heaven by spending quality time in God's presence. It is in our nature to find excuses to stay where we are in an unsettling place because it is familiar and safe. This is not the nature of our Father God. Psalm 86:10 says, "For thou art great, and doest wondrous things: Thou art God alone."

David was a man after God's own heart, and he committed many sins. Yet he was not afraid to seek the presence of God because he understood that fear immobilized him. This is a quote that will help you align your time with a proper perspective:

"Imagine you had a bank that each morning credited your account with $1,440—with one condition: whatever part of the $1,440 you failed to use during the day would be erased from your account, and no balance would be carried over. What would you do?"[6]

You do have this, and it's called time! There are 1,440 minutes in a day, and our Father has given them to us to be used for His good purpose.

To see the big picture is to see God and His plan for our lives. If we can't or just don't want to see it, we will not be able to have the right perspective about time. We will continue to go around the same mountain of "you win some, you lose some." With Christ, even when it feels like you've lost, you still win. But when you lose without Christ, you are lost.

Chapter 5
SAYING NO WITHOUT GUILT

"For I will give you a mouth and wisdom, which all your adversaries shall not be able to gainsay nor resist."
Luke 21:15

We are a spirit which desires the good and pure things from heaven. From the beginning, God has desired a relationship of love with us through communication. This leads to the perfect intimacy between God and us. Ask Him to help you in this area, if it is not already in place. Let this not be said of us:

> *"I got up early one morning*
> *and rushed right into the day.*
> *I had so much to accomplish*
> *that I didn't have time to pray."* [7]

Luke 21:15 reminds me of when I was diagnosed with breast cancer in 2018. My first response to the doctor as she gave me the report was, "Ok, thank you." My second response was, "God, what do I do with this? Do I believe it and what comes with it, or do I believe You?"

His answer was, "You are to believe both Me and it."

I was very reluctant to ask the next question, which was, "How do You want me go through this?"

His answer was chemo, and I was totally not in agreement with this answer. My heart was searching for a way out almost like Jesus before He went to the cross when He went to the Garden of Gethsemane. That day, I felt the same agony of the anticipation of this poison going into my body.

STRENGTH FROM WITHIN

Prayer is essential to our relationship with God. Jesus can relate to any situation that comes in our life; therefore, He is the perfect example to follow. I experienced a lot of sorrow alone as Jesus did until I finally looked to a friend for comfort and support. He was very attentive in listening to my pain being expressed through my words. Then with the power of God guiding his words, he said, "Trust the process."

At that very moment, everything in me stood still. The tears stopped. My heart was calm, and my mind was sound. My soul came into agreement with God's answer for chemo treatment. Previously, I never had to believe God for anything life-threatening concerning my health. I had surgery in the past, and I was very afraid, but I also didn't have a relationship with the Lord at that time. The fear I displayed in the past came from me.

The surgeon surprisingly took great steps making sure fear was not going to be a hinderance in my moving forward. He planned a pre-surgery visit a week in advance. He arranged for me to meet the staff who would be assisting him in surgery. He gave me a tour from admissions to the actual surgery room. All my fears subsided, and I began to trust the process.

This same fear was trying to come back into my life seventeen years later. The difference this time is that God, the great Physician, gave me the tour of safety.

It is time we face our fears and rise.

> *"Problems just tumbled about me*
> *and heavier came each task.*
> *'Why doesn't God help me?'*
> *He answered, 'You didn't ask.'"* [8]

When we experience deliverance, our minds transform from slaves of sin to sons of God. We have been redeemed from the curse of the law and we are now under grace which transforms us from the inside out. Grace doesn't mean we are free from oppositions, but it means we are free in oppositions.

JOY IN TRIALS

We must give our fears to God.

> *"I wanted to see joy and beauty,*
> *but the day toiled on gray and bleak.*
> *I wondered why God didn't show me.*
> *He said, 'But you didn't seek.'"* [9]

Trials will continue to come, but we get to see them from a different perspective. Our willingness and humility to make God's Word the standard for our lives leads to a healthy renewing of our minds. As we stop blaming others for our circumstances or for our negative thinking, God will start working on us in a powerful way.

When I have shared my story with others, some have said, "I've never heard a person say that God told them to go through chemo."

My response for me was, "He did, and I am standing here as a living testimony of His desired result."

A friend from church suggested I explore the cancer treatment center, and that is where amazing things started to manifest. I had meditated and believed the promises of God concerning the signs, wonders, and miracles following the believers. During my cancer journey, all three of those things were revealed. We often ask things of God, and we have no idea how He will bring them to light.

First, I asked God to retire me from working a nine to five secular job. Second, I was given a date to be released from Virginia after 27 years. I am now consistently growing in faith for what He has for my life in order to help others. This all transpired while going through chemo. Asking God for help during trials may sometimes lead to Him asking you to trust someone by sharing your situation with another of His choosing and then the truth of life is revealed.

The wonder of the Holy Spirit was in leading me to research every side effect and using Scripture to counteract it through commands. The command for the chemo was, "You are to go in and kill the cancer and come out," and "you will not damage any organ or any other parts of this body."

Every week I took a hot Epson salt bath to help pull the toxins out of my body. For every side effect that appeared, my doctor wanted to give me medication to combat it, but I declined. I asked God what I should do to combat this intruder, and each time, He gave me an answer. I followed every word of instruction given to me and believed in the power of God to bring about healing. Today, my health and strength are better than before this happened.

This trial was an opportunity to water and watch all the healing scriptures grow in God's increase. For years, I have been speaking healing scriptures over myself and didn't know why. The Word says that the Holy Spirit will intercede for us when we don't know how to pray.

POSITIONED TO RECEIVE

We often want the desired result of what we are asking for without doing the work. Trusting God is work, and it takes practice. We have a responsibility of growing in faith by the Word. We must trust what He gives us as the answer to what we need. When there is no doubt in our mind and no fear in our heart, growth will occur in trusting Him. "But without faith it's impossible to please him [God]…" (Hebrews 11:6).

This involves getting a clear conscience. We must take responsibility for every one of our thoughts, words, and actions (Acts 24:16, 2 Corinthians 10:3-6). We can obtain a clear conscience by taking every thought captive under Jesus's authority. It is written that the Word of God is living and powerful, and using God's Word is the only way to ward off these thoughts. Meditating on scriptures daily can be our source of life if we make a sincere, consistent commitment to it and not as an obligation.

> *"I tried to come into his presence.*
> *I used all my keys at the lock.*
> *God gently and lovingly chided,*
> *'My child, you didn't knock.'"* [10]

All our confidence comes from God, and with this confidence we can see in a storm. If we are really seeking Him, then this is where we should begin by saying "no" to doubt and unbelief and "yes" to God's promises. Saying "no" to fear, intimidation, and living a defeated life and saying "yes" to the abundant life of Jesus!

WE ALL NEED SOMEONE

The worst thing about treatment is not going through it but coming out of it. How you prepare for treatment is just as important as how you recover. Taking time to heal is vital. You must allow for that time, or you will overdo it.

Everybody needs a support person when facing a trial concerning their health. Everything surrounding this ordeal was guided by the Lord's hand. Months before I was diagnosed, He moved my youngest daughter home. She was there from the beginning to the end of the process.

My son went with me on some of my appointments, and I knew he was terrified, but he didn't show it. And my other daughter lives in Georgia where my treatment was set up. I could not have made this perfect plan by myself if I tried, but God is the perfect planner. We must trust Him.

As women, we often want to go through things like this alone, but we know deep in our heart it isn't good for us to be alone. I am blessed that my children come along side me during any stage in my life.

THE PROMISE KEEPER

After the flood and the rain had ceased, Noah sent a dove from the ark to see if there was dry land. The dove returned with an olive branch in its beak. A new beginning was just over the horizon.

Hope is a feeling of expectation, and a desire for a certain thing to happen. In other words, it's another way of trusting. God promised Noah and his family a new life as He has with us after we are born again. Noah sent the dove not once but three times.

God gives us more than one chance to get the understanding we need. After each lesson learned, there is a blessing on the other side. Be patient with yourself, and that same patience will bless someone else later.

> *"I woke up early this morning*
> *and paused before entering the day.*
> *I had so much to accomplish*
> *that I had to take time to pray."* [11]

Chapter 6
DARE TO DO SOMETHING DIFFERENT

"Though I speak with the tongues of men and of angels, and have not charity, I am become as sounding brass, or a tinkling cymbal. And though I have the gift of prophecy, and understand all mysteries, and all knowledge; and though I have all faith, so that I could remove mountains, and have not charity, I am nothing. And though I bestow all my goods to feed the poor, and though I give my body to be burned, and have not charity, it profiteth me nothing."
1 Corinthians 13:1-3

We often do not like to admit our weaknesses. I can remember a time when my heart was so wounded that I couldn't trust myself making any decisions. The poor choices I made in the past left me paralyzed, and making no decision felt better than making another mistake.

Our minds will tell us to keep doing the same thing and circumstances will get better. This thinking leads to insanity. It keeps us confused and going nowhere. We must say no to it and to the things of this world that tempt us to go against our Father God. Every sin we commit is against God. In the moment, we might think the decision only affects us, but we are wrong.

Most of us think we must be changed before Jesus will accept us, but this is another form of deception. Hiding our weaknesses only gives power to our adversary. It creates imaginative thoughts that go against the creative works of God. We must refuse it!

Positive thinking is good, and we can make some progress using it, but we were created to do great things. Therefore, it will take more than positive thinking in understanding what the Father's plan is to fulfill our lives.

When God calls us out from where we were, it is not to keep us from having fun or enjoying life. He is calling us to a more abundant life. Letting go of what is familiar to us is challenging but is always necessary.

To embrace change, we must be willing to leave all excuses behind to receive what's ahead and sometimes these include negative or abusive people. "Let go and let God" doesn't mean you don't care about these people; it shows you care about yourself. To overcome shame, guilt, and confusion we must come to Jesus just as we are—broken.

For any relationship to be reconciled, both parties involved must sacrifice. Many times, only one person does the sacrificing while the other reaps the benefits. In our case, God sacrificed His son, Jesus, for us to be reconciled to Him.

DO WHAT YOU ALREADY KNOW

There are many different opportunities for us as Christians to serve Christ in our community and the church. Our service must begin with honest, open-hearted prayer and personal one-on-one time with God. The more we invest in our relationship with Him the more we will understand how much we need Him. We need His guiding through the power of the Holy Spirit to accomplish anything that pleases Him.

One of the most important choices I made was the service of interceding in prayer for others. We pray for ourselves and our family members on a regular basis and sometimes still get up feeling heavy. But when we pray for others, it takes the focus off our circumstances, and we can then see the needs of someone else. Meanwhile, the Lord is blessing them and us through our service of prayer.

There is always someone out there whose problems are way worse than ours. Prayer is a ministry designed to keep us in constant communication with God. Then we will know the Father's heart without a doubt, and this moves us in position as sons of God (Romans 8:19). Prayer pleases God. It is written in Proverbs 16:7, "when a man's ways please the LORD, he maketh even his enemies to be at peace with him."

RELEASE EVERY SITUATION TODAY

Not every negative situation is from an outside enemy. There is an enemy within that needs to be acknowledged (Jeremiah 17:9). Our physical heart is actually a living, thinking organ. When our heart is wounded, it effects our decision-making process.

The heart possesses a "heart brain" composed of about 40,000 neurons that sense, feel, learn and remember. The heart brain sends messages to the head brain about how the body feels and more.[12]

DARE TO DO SOMETHING DIFFERENT

Negative emotions or states of mind can increase the risk for heart issues including irregular heart rhythms.[13] "Positive emotions create increased harmony and coherence in the heart rhythms and improve balance in the nervous system."[14]

"Disharmony in the nervous system leads to inefficiency and increased stress on the heart and other organs..." The heart is far more than a simple pump. "The heart is, in fact, a highly complex, self-organized information processing center with its own functional 'brain' that communicates..."[15] To boil it all down, the heart's influence on the body ultimately determines our quality of life.

Nelson Mandela is a great source of inspiration for us regarding how to deal with the matters of the heart. President Mandela left us with many heart-inspiring quotes. I believe this is appropriate for the time we are in now. "Everyone can rise above their circumstances and achieve success if they are dedicated to and passionate about what they do."[16]

Pain can be productive. Mandela, who himself came out of a terrible situation, was able to make a huge difference in his country. He didn't incite violence or lead people into starting riots. Instead, he calls for positive change and encouraged peace to the storm that he knew was brewing.

LOVE NEVER FAILS

He possessed love for God, love for his people and country, and love for himself. We often think if we love ourselves that it is selfish, but it's not true. Luke 6:32 says, "For if ye love them which love you, what thank have ye? For sinners also love those that love them." In other words it's easy to love those who love you, but we tend to stay away from those who we think are unlovable.

It takes work to love others, especially those who have walls and barriers up around them. This may be a challenge, but it is possible if we allow God to help us look past the outer exterior of the person's heart. If He shows you something about a person that is not of His light, it is for you to help them.

Prayer is often done in the secret place with our Father and in the name of Jesus. You might be the only one praying for that person. Someone must step up to the challenge, and that someone might be you. The true love of God is not conditional. We can't just turn it on and off like a faucet, nor can we pick or choose who to love whenever we feel like it.

DARE TO DO SOMETHING DIFFERENT

Leaders are called to love and to teach others how to love, and many of us can't fulfill this call because we do not understand that real love is God. Whatever excuses we have convinced ourselves of as to why we can't love another person are not from God.

"Charity suffereth long, and is kind; charity envieth not; charity vaunteth not itself, is not puffed up, doth not behave itself unseemly, seeketh not her own, is not easily provoked, thinketh no evil; rejoiceth not in iniquity, but rejoiceth in the truth; beareth all things, believeth all things, hopeth all things, endureth all things. Charity never faileth…" (1 Corinthians 13:4-8).

I have discovered in all my searches in life that I was created to love and be loved. This is the greatest fulfillment of all, and it begins with loving Jesus first. As I have stated before, Jesus is the only way to the Father. We cannot receive anything from God unless it comes through Jesus. We can acquire things and promotions through striving in our own strength, but they will not last without understanding God as our source.

Anything in our lives other than a healthy, balanced relationship with God and Jesus as our Savior is only a substitute for the real thing. Fulfillment is not just about feeling happy with your life choices, it is using all your creative ability to become the best you can be by serving others. Fulfilment is knowing that God's love is eternal and then trusting Him with our here and now.

God promises us that whoever believes in His son Jesus will be saved and shall not be ashamed (Romans 10:10-11). We've all made promises we didn't end up keeping, but it is not God's nature to break His word. We make promises to Him as a negotiation strategy. We do not have to make promises to God even if we intend on keeping them. Just be real and honest with Him because He knows every move we are going to take. Just trust Him and let Him make them with you.

Trust is only acquired through honesty and truth. When you accept truth in any situation, trust starts to develop. Denial is the worst place you can be in a relationship. It hinders any possible progress. Allowing yourself to continue to believe a lie will lead to destruction in any relationship. Only the truth makes you free. Accepting the truth frees you no matter how much it hurts.

Chapter 7
THE COURAGE TO CHANGE

"Being confident of this very thing, that he which hath begun a good work in you will perform it until the day of Jesus Christ."
Philippians 1:6

The book of our lives, written by God, is in heaven already. Each of our courses is already mapped out. He knows when we stop, go, or slow down on this journey. He desires is to commune with us daily in quality time. We are called to hear God's voice with our spirit and obey what is being spoken to us.

God has a plan for each of our lives, and He trusts us to cooperate with Him in completing it. There are people waiting for you to take your place in the kingdom of God. Only you have what it takes to help them overcome the challenges in their lives. Everyone wants to know that someone cares. Helping free others from emotional distress helps them move forward with joy. There is nothing impossible with God (Matthew 19:26).

Our role is to help create a desire in others to become better because of God's presence being our number one priority. The impact of God's presence is so powerful that even when we don't feel His presence, we know He is still there. When we solely rely on Him for our every move, we will discover His will for our lives (Matthew 6:10).

THE SPIRIT WHO LEADS

If we actually loved God the way we say we do, obedience would not be a problem such as it is today (John 14:15). We can effectively overcome disobedience by eliminating the distraction that is causing us to lose focus in this area. We often tend to run from opposition, but it will meet us at our next destination until it is confronted and taken authority over.

The Holy Spirit was sent to us to help give us guidance and each of our outcomes will be different, but they are brought about by the same Spirit (John 16:13).

Once we decide to resist opposition, clear distractions, and intentionally become focused, we will be able to hear God's instructions clearly and find the solution. Just a reminder that once we decided to follow Jesus Christ, we entered into an agreement where quitting is not an option (1 Corinthians 10:13).

Everything is built on the principle of God's authority. He delegates authority to governmental officials, parents, spiritual gifts, and assignments. We must answer to Him for the way we used this authority and how we treated those under our care.

God directed authority to be used through His unconditional love. We are not to function from favoritism or partiality. Our position holds us accountable to teach what is moral and true through sound doctrine (2 Timothy 4).

TRUTH IN IDENTITY

Acceptance is hard to welcome when we are trying so hard to hold on to what we so desperately need to let go of. As we allow our unwanted private experiences (thoughts, feelings, and urges) to come and go without struggling with them, we will grow.

Our identity rests in who we are in spirit and in truth, not in what we can do. We are more than a daughter, a wife, or a mother. It's time we seek God for that "more than I can see" answer. We have been what others say we are long enough. Use what you already know to become who you already are in Christ!

Shift the atmosphere from expecting the worst to expecting the best. Open your heart to receive the gift of God's true understanding of the abundant life that He has given you. Be patient with yourself and keep a positive outlook, especially in what looks to be a bad situation. God's blessings are all around you, reach out and grab them. Make humor a daily regiment as an entrance to living in a lifetime of joy.

As we embrace God's truth of who He says we are, we become empowered to trust Him in the growing process. We are all necessary and important to God. Our significance and worth are something only He can bring into perspective for us. Stay connected to Him.

TRANSFORMED MIND

Jesus has everything we need to maintain a healthy relationship with the Father. He helps us gain fresh confidence, so we walk out His work passionately. His lifting voice reminds us of how wonderful we are because we are created in the image of God. He sees only God's perfection in each person in every situation and will help you do the same. He will teach us how to see ourselves as someone who is loved completely and unconditionally, just as we are.

We often hear people say, "It is what it is." What that means is we look to our circumstances as truth. Even when we are not trusting God, we are still putting our trust in something or someone either good or bad. There is no perfect start, so release every situation today.

Adam and Eve had to start over, and I'm sure the circumstances surrounding them were not ideal. Because of their sin, they had to leave the perfect environment, where they were comfortable, to create a new beginning. Even in new surroundings, God was still with them. They just weren't allowed to live in the garden.

But the mercy of God's grace covered them and with His instructions they obeyed. When we are given instructions, they are to be carried out exactly as they are given. It honors God when we are prepared to do anything He asks of us. We receive His peace as a blessing. Respond in a way that communicates your heart to both understand and to bring understanding.

Whatever you are going through is for you and for someone else because you were born with a purpose. God knew you before you were conceived. He placed in you everything you need to live for Him. Only you can hinder your progress. So take a stand and run with perseverance to the finish line. If you can see past the smoke screen of the adversary, you will see that greater is here!

> *"Our deepest fear is not that we are inadequate. Our deepest fear is that we are powerful beyond measure. It is our light, not our darkness that most frightens us. We ask ourselves, 'Who am I to be brilliant, gorgeous, talented, fabulous?' Actually, who are you not to be? You are a child of God. Your playing [it] small does not serve the world. There is nothing enlightened about shrinking so that other people won't feel insecure around you. We are all meant to shine, as children do. We were born to make manifest the glory of God that is within us. It's not just in some of us; it's in everyone. And as we let our light shine, we unconsciously give other people permission to do the same. As we are liberated from our own fear, our presence automatically liberates others."*[17]
>
> **MARIANNE WILLIAMSON**
> A Return to Love: Reflections on the Principles of "A Course in Miracles"

CONCLUSION

*"Failure is simply the opportunity to begin
again, this time more intelligently."*
Henry Ford [18]

Today is a new day. We don't have to live in the mistakes, failures, and disappointments of yesterday. We can choose to move forward. What we do today helps create our tomorrow. Every day we have a choice, so what will we choose? We must be patient with ourselves. Remember every trial is an opportunity to grow in faith, and faith is what we need to please God.

Look for the good in every moment, especially the hard times. If we don't see it, we can become it! Trust the power of God in who He says we are, because now is the time. Stop putting things off and have faith in the reality of who we are becoming. We must believe that we are more than conquerors, and we can do this.

about the author

Dolores Jones is the founder of the transformation healing brand—A Mind 2 Work. She has dedicated her life to inspiring, encouraging, and empowering women of all walks of life.

Dolores has had many opportunities to quit. The life she chose to live for Christ was worth more than the pain she had to let go of in exchange for necessary growth. Her motto has become, "Quitting is not an option!"

Serving God with a sincere heart is Dolores's passion, combined with her goal of helping others find joy while developing a loving relationship with Jesus.

Nothing brings her more fulfillment than witnessing the power of God, replacing the label of a wounded heart from victim to victorious.

ENDNOTES

1   "Opposition Definition & Meaning." Merriam-Webster, Merriam-Webster, https://www.merriam-webster.com/dictionary/opposition.

2   "Enduring Definition." Enduring Definitions | What Does Enduring Mean? | Best 6 Definitions of Enduring, https://www.yourdictionary.com/enduring.

3   Hornblower, Simon, et al. "Reverence." The Oxford Classical Dictionary, Oxford University Press, 2012.

4   "G1754 - Energeō - Strong's Greek Lexicon (KJV)." Blue Letter Bible, https://www.blueletterbible.org/lexicon/g1754/kjv/tr/0-1/.

5   "Deception Definition & Meaning." Dictionary.com, Dictionary.com, https://www.dictionary.com/browse/deception.

6 Landers, Ann. "Imagine You Had a Bank That Each Morning Credited Your Account with $1,440." IdleHearts, https://www.idlehearts.com/2217824/imagine-you-had-a-bank-that-each-morning-credited-your-account-with-1440.

7 Grant, Alan. "The Difference." Scrapbook.com, https://www.scrapbook.com/poems/doc/33747.html.

8 Ibid.

9 Ibid.

10 Ibid.

11 Ibid.

12 AM, Alshami. "Pain: Is It All in the Brain or the Heart?" Current Pain and Headache Reports, U.S. National Library of Medicine, https://pubmed.ncbi.nlm.nih.gov/31728781/#:~:text=Armour%2C%20in%201991%2C%20discovered%20that,has%20its%20own%20nervous%20system. .

13 https://www.eehealth.org/blog/2019/03/emotions-heart-health/

14 "Science of the Heart." HeartMath Institute, https://www.heartmath.org/resources/downloads/science-of-the-heart/.

ENDNOTES

15 Ibid.

16 "15 Nelson Mandela Quotes." Encyclopædia Britannica, Encyclopædia Britannica, Inc., https://www.britannica.com/list/nelson-mandela-quotes#:~:text=%E2%80%9CEveryone%20can%20rise%20above%20their,passionate%20about%20what%20they%20do.%E2%80%9D

17 "A Quote from a Return to Love." Goodreads, Goodreads, https://www.goodreads.com/quotes/928-our-deepest-fear-is-not-that-we-are-inadequate-our.

18 Quotespedia.org. "Failure Is Simply the Opportunity to Begin Again, This Time More..." Quotespedia.org, 8 Apr. 2020, https://www.quotespedia.org/authors/h/henry-ford/failure-is-simply-the-opportunity-to-begin-again-this-time-more-intelligently-henry-ford/.

Made in the USA
Middletown, DE
12 September 2023

38122865R00046